FINDING A PATH
THROUGH DIFFICULT TIMES

To par Excellence —

Thank you for all your help,

Anthony L. Sardella

ANTHONY L. SARDELLA

author**HOUSE**®

AuthorHouse™
1663 Liberty Drive
Bloomington, IN 47403
www.authorhouse.com
Phone: 1-800-839-8640

Published by AuthorHouse   03/16/2013

ISBN: 978-1-4817-2359-6 (sc)
ISBN: 978-1-4817-2358-9 (e)

Library of Congress Control Number: 2013904113

This book is printed on acid-free paper.

CONTENTS

Acknowledgments vii
Introduction.. ix
1. Finding a Path 1
2. Feeling Broken...................................5
3. Holding On...................................9
4. Sometimes There Are No Answers 13
5. Seeking Guidance 17
6. Facing Our Fears...................................21
7. Hope and Faith.................................25
8. Forgiveness 29
9. Finding Purpose Again...........................33
10. Seeking Balance..................................37
11. Patience 41
12. Finding Grace.....................................45
13. Opportunity 49
14. Spiritual Footprints 53
15. The Caregiver.....................................57
16. Life Is Ever Changing.............................61
17. The Road Ahead...................................65
18. It's Just a Dress 69
19. Finding Your Own Path...........................73
20. Your Journey 75

To my wife and children, who have brought so much love and kindness into my life. They helped me become the person I am today.

Acknowledgments

I would like to thank my sons, Anthony and Michael—Anthony for his help in formatting the book and Michael for his ideas and support. Thanks also to Joseph Angerone for designing the book cover; to Linda and Nick Pasquarello for their guidance throughout this process; to Doreen Murphy for editing and giving me clarity about the theme of the book; and to the ladies at Par Excellence who put up with my handwriting. Finally, my thanks to the rest of my family and friends who contributed their ideas and support for this book.

The cover picture was taken at Holmdel Park in New Jersey by Anthony L. Sardella.

*All profits from this book will go to charitable organizations.

INTRODUCTION

I started writing as an outlet for myself after I had gone through some challenging times that changed my life forever. Trying to find a path through a difficult time was not an easy thing to do. Writing gave me comfort and clarity about what had happened. As my writing continued, I decided to turn it into a book so that others may benefit from my experiences.

Everyone at some point in his or her life will experience some kind of life-changing event. Although there might not seem to be any light when first faced with adversity, be assured there will be better days ahead. It will take time, patience, courage, and strength to be able to find a path that will open our hearts and allow us to find peace within.

1

FINDING A PATH

It's funny how life takes us on journeys we're not ready for, but from time to time the road we are on begins to bend and curve. We find that the path we had been on is no longer visible. At that point, we may discover we're lost. It can happen to anyone at any given time. This is inevitable; no one is exempt.

Many times when we face difficulties, it feels like we are caught up in a storm. Life offers us many challenges that we must face on a daily basis—work, stress, emotional and physical issues, financial and family problems, and ultimately, at some point, dealing with the death of a loved one. All of these challenges are scary and even overwhelming; it may feel like we are lost at sea with no land in sight. Each day we have to face uncertainty, and often we must face these challenges alone, even if there are people around to help guide us.

When we're caught in one of these "storms," we confront many emotions that we are not always used to dealing with: anxiety, panic, fear, and shock. With no beacon in sight, we have to face a new landscape, one we've never seen before. Trying to navigate these new waters is uncomfortable and uncertain, and we yearn for the landscape we had before.

As we find ourselves on a new path, we try to make sense of what happened. How did we get here? Trying to put the pieces back together will be a daunting task. Every person has his or her own path to take and cross to bear. As time goes on, we have to let go of what has happened, even though it seems surreal at times. We can surrender to it and stop fighting it in our mind—which is easier said than done. All of us have different levels of emotional sensitivity. It may take one person a short time to adjust to things, while it may take another person much longer. There is no timeline or race that we have to finish; we will get there when we are ready. This is when we realize it is comforting to know that we already have the pieces of the puzzle; it's just a matter of time before we sort through them. Realizing that we have to live in the present moment, to live for today, feels liberating.

Whether we're still caught up in a storm or surveying the damage in the aftermath, it is important to avoid making any hasty decisions. We must give ourselves time to conceptualize and understand what has happened to us. Trying to put all the pieces back together again very quickly could put us on a path that we may regret. When we make hasty decisions, they usually are the wrong ones. Living with uncertainty is very difficult to deal with. However, there are times when we have no other choice.

Does time heal all wounds? That is sometimes a very difficult question to answer. There will always be unexpected reminders of all the hurt we have gone through. As time does go by and we heal, we will find ourselves stronger, because we survived and had no choice but to fight our way through our adversity. No matter what path we take, it is important, both emotionally and physically, to be positive and to take care of our bodies. Eating right and exercising is crucial to healing, even though it may be difficult to do, especially when our minds stray. It's easy to imagine so many scenarios again and again, and to constantly worry. A life coach I worked with while going through a storm of my own had an interesting saying about worrying: "When we worry, we are imagining something we don't want to happen—so don't do it."

It is often difficult to ride out a storm on our own. It is perfectly fine to lean on others and to seek help if needed. Finding help does not mean we are weak; it's just the opposite. We are trying to get our lives back together again. But often we must take a "time-out," whether to relax or to reflect upon what has transpired. Taking time to rejuvenate and refresh ourselves is not a selfish thing to do; it helps us and the people closest to us, because we will be able to think more clearly and deal with people in a more relaxed way. Also, helping others while going through a difficult time can open our hearts and make us feel better, because it allows us to take the focus off of ourselves and refocus on others in a positive way.

Many of us will turn to religion when things start to fall apart. Going to a place of worship for guidance and prayer is very beneficial. Offering up all hurt and sorrow to our Creator can provide us with a sense of grace and peacefulness that we can carry with us. Everyone has the ability to achieve inner peace, which is inherent in all of us.

We will face many challenges in our lifetime and will have many new paths to follow. There will be obstacles to overcome and opportunities to be had. Each path we take brings us closer to ourselves with greater understanding. We will find the road we are on to be more manageable now, yet ever changing.

2

FEELING BROKEN

There are times in our lives that we may feel broken, whether it is from a loss of a loved one, divorce, loss of a job, and so forth. Our spirit is lost. As we grieve from a loss, it takes us on a path in which we feel little hope. We get a sense of feeling alone as we go down this dark road. It is very difficult to live every day with the pain and suffering that we are carrying with us. Doing our daily activities gets more challenging as each day passes.

Trying to break free from the troubles we are having takes time and patience. Just as when we get a cut, it takes time to heal. The deeper the wound, the longer it takes to feel better. We need to take care of ourselves in order to heal. Allowing ourselves the time to recover is extremely important to our mental and physical health. Eventually, when we accept and surrender to what is in front of us by letting go and not holding on to the pain we experienced, we can lift our hearts and recapture our human spirit.

Facing adversity shows us how much strength we really have.

3

HOLDING ON

A life-changing event often comes as a shock. Some may have had time to prepare for it, while others may have not. No one is ever truly ready to handle a tragedy in front of them. Trying to make sense of what just transpired is too difficult. A person may feel like they lost their lifejacket while being caught up in a storm. Staying afloat with no guiding beacon is overwhelming; each breath and each minute seems like an eternity. There is no set way to stay afloat. We need to figure that out ourselves.

When confronted with a tragedy, we need to tap into our inner strength and faith to help us get through it. As time passes, we can't imagine how we got through our circumstances. Everyone has an innate fighter within to help survive—taking it one moment and one step at a time will help us bridge the seconds, the minutes, hours, and days together, and eventually we will be able to find that there is hope with better days ahead. Taking it one moment at a time enables us to navigate the challenges we just faced.

Surrender your pain and your heart will be softened.

4

SOMETIMES THERE ARE NO ANSWERS

Trying to make sense of a tragedy or a very bad situation can be difficult to do; it may feel surreal and overwhelming. Even as time passes and we search for answers, we might not find what we are looking for. Accepting the idea that we may never find out why something happened can finally let us be free of the struggle within. Allowing ourselves to stop searching will give us more time to focus on the present moment, which will lighten our hearts and souls.

Knowing what tomorrow will bring can be even scarier than today.

5

SEEKING GUIDANCE

Most times we are able to handle adversity on our own. Accepting the idea that we may need help may make us feel weak, but there will be occasions when we need to reach out and get some guidance. When people get stuck, there are many places they can turn. Whether with a trusted friend, in a place of worship, or with a group or a professional, sharing suffering can help us open our hearts and see hope once again. We want to share with someone who is kind, caring, and compassionate. Reaching out to someone not only benefits us but also gives the other individual a great gift—the ability to help another person who is suffering. It takes time to heal, but with courage, strength, and guidance, the path that we are on now will become clearer and not as scary as the previous path we were traveling on.

Reaching out for help is not a sign of weakness in times of need, but of a sign of strength.

6

FACING OUR FEARS

O ne of the most difficult things to do in life is to face our fears. Being fearful of something can take a toll on both mind and body. Many of us will fall down in life; most often we will get up on our own, but there may be other times when we need a helping hand. We are all built unique. Everyone handles fear and uncertainty in his or her own way. Sometimes we are thrust into terrifying situations we are not prepared for. Anxiety and panic come to the forefront when this happens. It may happen many times in a lifetime; sometimes we face our fear, while other times we may not.

Facing our fears requires courage, strength, and a strategy to help us through them. Each of us needs to come up with our own plan. Developing a plan may take some trial and error, but ultimately, as long as we keep on trying, we will overcome our fears and have a more fulfilling life. Taking it one step at a time, looking at fear as an opportunity to grow, facing it head-on, seeking help, and praying or meditating are some ways that can help. Fear is essentially just not wanting to face something unfamiliar; the more we learn about and accept our fears, the less scary they become.

Fear can be an opportunity or a feeling of despair; it's up to us to decide.

7

HOPE AND FAITH

When confronted with an overwhelming situation, we may feel like we are staring into an abyss with no way out. Life seems surreal to us, as we just go through the motions of what is happening. Looking for a light at the end of a tunnel that we cannot see brings us to a point of despair.

Living without hope in our hearts can be quite scary and very challenging. Being able to believe in a positive outcome is one of many steps in bringing back hope into our hearts. Trying to find peace in our lives while going through adversity, we must consider the reality of what is in front of us while having faith that we will be okay in whatever life brings us. Even though we manage our expectations of events that may follow, it is uplifting to know that there will be better times ahead. Whether we turn to a higher power or something positive that gives us hope, navigating through the labyrinth we are in will eventually lead us to a peaceful heart.

Having the courage, which is in all of us, will give us strength and guidance while being confronted with difficult times. Having hope and faith in ourselves will give us more peace and harmony to maintain the delicate balance of the life we live. Knowing that there will be a tomorrow, makes today more manageable, and enables us to live in the present moment. Hope taps the light inside us that guides us through the difficulties that we may face in life.

Hope is the light that will guide us through the dark.

8

FORGIVENESS

One of the hardest things to do is to forgive, whether ourselves or others. Some people carry this hurt with them for years. Doing so affects us, mind, body, and soul, in so many different ways. Being mad over a past outcome is all-consuming and a waste of energy and time. Allowing the hurt to leave us will bring us greater joy and peace.

Forgiving someone for something they said or did benefits both parties. Being freed from hatred and suffering can allow ourselves to open our hearts and live life with more meaning. Once we forgive, we will feel less burdened and have more compassion for others. No one is perfect; we all make mistakes. Giving forgiveness to yourself or others is a blessing for all.

Forgiveness is the seed of a lightened heart.

9

FINDING PURPOSE AGAIN

Pushing ahead when confronted with a life-changing event can be quite difficult. It takes courage and strength to keep moving forward while trying to find meaning again. Life will never be the same, and the uncertainty of the future can be overwhelming. Most times we do not have a compass to help us navigate through this difficult time. We will no longer have our ducks in a row; they will be scattered for a while. This will allow us time to figure out what comes next and to be open to what it is. It's fine not having all the answers to what's to follow. We will acclimate our minds, bodies, and souls over time to help us navigate the new road we are on. Letting go of the difficult times will help us find our purpose again. Life will again have greater meaning to us, and we will be able to live more in the present moment. Having life with meaning will give us greater joy and hope for a better tomorrow.

*We can never fully lose the
pieces of the puzzle that is our
life, because they are forever
in our hearts.*

10

SEEKING BALANCE

As we continue our journey in life, it is important to seek balance. Finding a new way to juggle all of our responsibilities and commitments is very challenging. We often make excuses about why we cannot find the time to do the things we want to do. We are cheating ourselves and the people we care about if we do not keep on trying. If seeking balance is difficult to do, that indicates that our lifestyle needs to change. It may take many attempts, but eventually our lives will seem more manageable.

Finding time for ourselves is extremely important, both mentally and physically. Exercising gives us the opportunity to become more fit, which helps us in many ways. Our energy levels will increase and weight will be more stable. Eating right also plays a role on how we feel. If we eat junk, our body will feel sluggish and will be more prone to getting sick. A balanced diet will take us in the right direction in helping us try to find balance.

Meditation and prayer can give us greater understanding on how to find the equilibrium that we are seeking. There is no set way to pray or meditate; people have to do what is most comfortable for them. By meditating, we will see ourselves become a calmer and more peaceful person by doing so. Setting out time every day, whether it's five minutes or one hour, is very important. It may be trying at first, but eventually it becomes a part of our daily lives.

There are many sources we could tap into to find greater balance. It will be trial and error at times. Healing our mind and body may take time, but with persistence, the new path that we are on will be brighter. However, once we find greater understanding of ourselves and life, there will always be challenges ahead that will test us. Being more centered makes the task of finding stability again easier, because of the wisdom that we have picked up on our journey.

Balance is the key to harmony.

11

PATIENCE

When going through tough times, it is very easy to lose patience. We want everything to be over and settled, so we can get back to everyday life. Riding out a storm is no easy task, especially if we see the storm ahead of us. We can prepare for it, but unless we have traveled this road before, we will be very anxious about what to expect. We all have a different level of patience, but wanting to resolve a situation before it is over can be detrimental to the outcome. Having the ability to get through adversity will take perseverance and strength. We could all use more patience for ourselves and others. Practicing patience, whatever method we use, before something bad happens will give us the ability to cope better when dealt a life-changing event. We can practice having more patience every day, whether we are waiting in a long line or helping someone who does things slower than we do. With time, we will see that our patience has improved. Staying with something that is uncomfortable for a stretch of time eventually will become easier. Going through the process is the most difficult part. When things become more settled in our lives, we will be amazed at how we were able to get through it.

As much as we rush in life, we will never get to where we want to be unless we slow down.

12

FINDING GRACE

As we continue with our journey, there will be moments that we feel a sense of calmness and a state of well-being. It may feel like the stars are aligned and everything is right with the world. This feeling of grace warms our heart and soul. Allowing ourselves to surrender to what lies in front of us and to let go of what happens next can lift the huge weight that is sitting on our shoulders. Accepting the idea that we cannot change things frees us from the bonds that we put on ourselves. Grace can open our hearts to the pain and suffering that we're feeling. This sense of peace in our life will enable us to move forward. Even in the midst of darkness we can tap into our faith and inner strength to find peace.

Grace can be found even in the darkest of places.

13

OPPORTUNITY

There will be times in our life when we have to deal with adversity. It is extremely hard to turn off all those emotions we are feeling when faced with a devastating situation, but with patience and time we will be able to see how adversity can make us a stronger person and how we will be able to use our experiences to help others.

Leaning into adversity can strengthen our soul. Being able to survive the circumstances that life puts in front of us is courageous and rewarding. It may take time to overcome obstacles, but with these experiences comes greater strength. The knowledge that we gain through difficult times can open our hearts to others that are experiencing their own challenges. Being able to bring balance to another person is quite rewarding. It helps both us and the person in need.

Turning adversity into opportunity will give us strength to help others.

14

SPIRITUAL FOOTPRINTS

While many of us today are trying to peacefully coexist with the earth, in which we are mindful of our carbon footprint, it is just as important to be aware of our spiritual footprints. As we live every day with our busy lives, it is easy to forget about how interconnected we all are. When something happens to one person, it will impact the lives of many others.

Following a path of spiritual well-being is one of many steps we could take individually. Creating peace and harmony with others is vital to the world we live in. Making a conscious effort to live a life with an open heart and loving kindness will benefit all of society.

Spirituality is innate in all of us; it lies within our spirit, whether we are religious or not. Everyone can become a spiritual person. It is crucial, in today's world, that we connect with ourselves as well as with others. Being able to connect with the human spirit can be a transforming experience that nourishes our souls and liberates our existence. The benefits are numerous: better health, peacefulness, and a greater sense of self.

If we do not refuel spiritually,
we will run out of gas.

16

LIFE IS EVER CHANGING

As we plan for the future, we set goals. Most times, however, life does not play out the way we want it to. We may face adversity many times within our lives; it may feel as if we are swimming against the tide with no relief in sight, as we become tired, fearful, and concerned about what lies ahead. Embracing the idea that life is impermanent and accepting the fact that life is fluid can give us greater understanding and strength.

Sometimes we need to step back and take a time-out from our busy lives. It is normal to feel stuck at times; it is an opportunity to reassess where we are and where we are going. During such times, it is important to make adjustments in our lives to achieve greater balance.

As we become more balanced, we will come to a path of greater knowledge, and we will be able to handle and accept the various changes that life offers us. The incessant internal chatter will ease, and a feeling of grace will envelop us, allowing our hearts to lighten and make us more aware of living in the present moment, and finally leading us to greater peace and happiness.

Life changes without our consent.

17

THE ROAD AHEAD

While there may be many challenges ahead of us, we get to write our next chapter. Not knowing what happens next can be scary but can also bring hope and joy. While we acclimate to our "new normal," living in the present moment, and not reliving the past or trying to predict the future, will help our minds to stop racing and allow us to live with happiness again. Knowing that we are not alone, and that others may be following a similar path with their own cross to bear, can give us a connection with others. As we continue our journey, it may seem like we are on a roller coaster at times, but eventually the path we are on will level out, and the road ahead will be filled with endless possibilities.

When we look back at the aftermath of what we once went through, we will find ourselves stronger and more mindful because of it. As the clouds clear, we begin to see a new sense of purpose and happiness. The future will take care of itself, and we should not worry about the things we cannot change.

*Embrace the road ahead;
it's filled with endless
possibilities.*

This inspirational personal essay was written by my wife, Lisa Ann Sardella. It was published by Central Jersey Family Magazine *in October 2008.*

18

IT'S JUST A DRESS

"It's just a dress." My husband said those words to me as I headed out the door in search of a dress to wear to a wedding. He was right, but at the time, buying this dress seemed like a monumental task. I was procrastinating, and it is not like me to put off shopping. I love to shop. I have absolutely no problem buying anything. But this was different.

I am a breast cancer survivor. I have been for about two years now. Nevertheless, this story is not about my cancer experience. There are millions of inspiring stories, and there is an entire sisterhood created by the great many of us who have battled those dark days. Instead, this is a story about "my dress" and how I regained my human spirit.

It all started last year when I had to find a dress for a different wedding. Finding an appropriate dress to accommodate my temporary breast form and the undergarment I needed to feel "normal" was quite a challenge. In fact, I have to say that the whole experience was dispiriting and frustrating. After several weeks of trying on countless dresses, I finally settled on something that the fashion police would have arrested me for wearing. It turned out that I never had to wear it, because our babysitter was sick

69

and I didn't go to the wedding. I stayed home and my husband went. (I was so relieved.) The next day I returned the outfit. I was never meant to be seen in public wearing it, and I must have known that deep down inside, since I had not removed any of the tags

Fast-forward, and perhaps you can understand why this year's trip in search of a dress was intimidating me. And yet so much had changed since last year. The healing process was well under way, and my breast reconstruction was now complete. Though my body was far from perfect, I was now living without the breast form (or "poof," as my kids referred to it) and, for that matter, going without a bra at all most of the time. One would think that I would be excited to shop this time around. But that last shopping expedition scarred me so much that I was dreading it.

I headed for a mall with large department stores, rather than trying the local boutiques. I figured that I could hide among the volume of clothes, and therefore not attract any attention from the salespeople. I wanted to shop as invisibly as possible.

I like to think that I am a strong-minded individual who can face most difficult situations head-on, but that was not how I felt. As I was driving to the mall, I kept thinking of my husband's words to me as I left home: "It's just a dress." But if he only knew how I was feeling! It was as if this experience would dictate how feminine I could ever feel again, or how "normal" I was now.

Then I started thinking about how many other people may have a symbolic "dress" in their life—something that may be bringing them down and crushing their inner strength or spirit. This stirred the fighter instinct inside of me, raising me up for the challenge. I entered the store with newfound energy. I kept telling myself, "You have been through so much more than this. You are a confident woman with two breasts now—albeit not perfect breasts. But whose are, anyway?"

My search started out slowly. I examined dress after dress, thinking how bad I would probably look in *this* one, or thinking *that* one was too revealing. The first ten or so I tried on were failures, but I did not get discouraged. Instead, I became hopeful. I left the fitting room with a better idea of what might look good on me—and then went for a second round. Finally I tried on a pretty halter dress, not a typical pick for me even before the cancer. That dress turned out to be the one. It looked good. I was comfortable and not self-conscious. This was a major accomplishment. So I did it—I made the purchase. When I went to the wedding, I felt great.

I share this story not to discuss my shopping experiences, but to offer hope and encouragement to any woman with something to overcome, or with "a dress" that is bringing her down. For me, I discovered that it was not just a dress that I needed to find, but my human spirit, my inner strength. And, I am happy to say, I found it while shopping for that dress.

Lisa lost her battle with breast cancer a year after this article was published.

19

FINDING YOUR OWN PATH

When we are going through a difficult time, our hearts may become heavy and our spirit lost. Trying to break free from these feelings can be quite challenging. However, there is something inside of us that pushes us to find happiness again.

Even though the lights of our hearts may dim, opening our hearts again to ourselves, family, community, and new relationships can bring about a brighter future that will give us peace and happiness in our lives again.

Your Journey

The next few pages are for you, if you want to take notes and to discover your own path to finding balance and harmony in your life.

_____

_____

_____

_____

_____

_____

_____

_____

_____

_____

_____

_____

_____

_____

_____

_____

_____

_____

_____

_____